HOW TO REPAIR THE WRONG YOU'VE DONE

The Living as a Christian Series:

Basic Christian Maturity

Growing in Faith
   Steve Clark
Knowing God's Will
   Steve Clark
Decision to Love
   Ken Wilson
God First
   Ken Wilson
Sons and Daughters of God
   Ken Wilson

Overcoming Obstacles to Christian Living

Getting Free
   Bert Ghezzi
How to Repair the Wrong You've Done
   Ken Wilson

The Emotions

The Angry Christian
   Bert Ghezzi
The Self-Image of a Christian
   Mark Kinzer
Living with a Clear Conscience
   Mark Kinzer

Christian Character

Strength Under Control
   John Keating
*How to Become the Person You
   Were Meant to Be*
   Peter Williamson

**Bert Ghezzi and Peter Williamson
General Editors**

How to Repair the Wrong You've Done

Steps to Restoring Relationships

Ken Wilson

SERVANT BOOKS
Ann Arbor, Michigan

Published by Servant Books
P.O. Box 8617
Ann Arbor, Michigan 48107

Cover Photo by John B. Leidy © 1982, Servant
Publications
Book Design by John B. Leidy

Scripture quotations are taken from the *Revised
Standard Version* of the Bible, copyrighted 1946, 1952
© 1971, 1973; the *New International Version,* copyright
© 1978 by New York International Bible Society, all
rights reserved; the *New American Standard Bible,*
copyright © 1960, 1962, 1963, 1968, 1971, 1972, 1973,
The Lockman Foundation, all rights reserved.

Printed in the United States of America.
ISBN 0-89283-116-2

Contents

Living as a Christian

IN HUMAN TERMS, it is not easy to decide to follow
Jesus Christ and to live our lives as Christians.
Jesus requires that we surrender our selves to him,
relinquish our aspirations for our lives, and submit
our will to God. Men and women have never been
able to do this easily; if we could, we wouldn't
need a savior.

Once we accept the invitation and decide to
follow Jesus, a new set of obstacles and problems
asserts itself. We find that we are often ignorant
about what God wants of us as his sons and
daughters. For example, what does it mean
practically to obey the first commandment—to
love God with our whole mind, heart, and
strength? How can we know God's will? How do
we love people we don't like? How does being a
Christian affect what we do with our time and
money? What does it mean "to turn the other
cheek?" In these areas—and many others—it is
not easy to understand exactly what God wants.

Even when we do know what God wants, it can
be quite difficult to apply his teaching to our daily
lives. Questions abound. How do we find time to

pray regularly? How do we repair a relationship with someone we have wronged or who has wronged us? How do we handle unruly emotional reactions? These are examples of perplexing questions about the application of Christian teaching to our daily lives.

Furthermore, we soon discover that Christians have enemies—the devil outside and the flesh within. Satan tempts us to sin; our inner urges welcome the temptation, and we find our will to resist steadily eroding.

Finally, we must overcome the world. We are living in an environment that is hostile toward what Christians believe and how they live, and friendly toward those who believe and do the opposite. The world in which we live works on our Christian resolve in many subtle ways. How much easier it is to think and act like those around us! How do we persevere?

There is a two-fold answer to these questions: To live successfully as Christians, we need both grace and wisdom. Both are freely available from the Lord to those who seek him.

As Christians we live by grace. The very life of God works in us as we try to understand God's teaching, apply it to our lives, and overcome the forces that would turn us aside from our chosen path. The grace we need is always there. The Lord is with us always, and the supply of his grace is inexhaustible.

Yet grace works with wisdom. Christians must *learn* a great deal about how to live according to

God's will. We must study God's word in scripture, listen to Christian teaching, and reflect on our own experience and the experience of others. Many Christians today lack this kind of wisdom. This is the need which the *Living as a Christian* series is designed to meet.

The book you are reading is part of a series of books intended to help Christians apply the teaching of scripture to their lives. The authors of *Living as a Christian* books are pastoral leaders who have given this teaching in programs of Christian formation in various Christian communities. The teaching has stood the test of time. It has already helped many people grow as faithful servants of the Lord. We decided it was time to make this teaching available in book form.

All the *Living as a Christian* books seek to meet the following criteria:

- **Biblical.** The teaching is rooted in scripture. The authors and editors maintain that scripture is the word of God, and that it ought to determine what Christians believe and how they live.

- **Practical.** The purpose of the series is to offer down-to-earth advice about living as a Christian.

- **Relevant.** The teaching is aimed at the needs we encounter in our daily lives—at home, in school, on the job, in our day-to-day relationships.

- **Brief and Readable.** We have designed the series for busy people from a wide variety of backgrounds. Each of the authors presents profound Christian truths as simply and clearly as possible, and illustrates those truths by examples drawn from personal experience.

- **Integrated.** The books in the series comprise a unified curriculum on Christian living. They do not present differing views, but rather they take a consistent approach.

The format of the series makes it suitable for both individual and group use. The books in *Living as a Christian* can be used in such group settings as Sunday school classes, adult education programs, prayer groups, classes for teenagers, women's groups, and as a supplement to Bible study.

The *Living as a Christian* series is divided into several sets of books, each devoted to a different aspect of Christian living. These sets include books on Christian maturity, emotions in the Christian life, the fruit of the Holy Spirit, Christian personal relationships, Christian service, and, very likely, on other topics as well.

This book, *How to Repair the Wrong You've Done*, is one of a set of books which will help you overcome obstacles to your growth in Christian maturity. Soon after making a serious commitment to the Lord, we usually become aware of things that hinder our growth—obstacles such as our own wrongdoing, the world, the flesh, and the devil. *How to Repair the Wrong You've Done* and other books in this set present practical, scripturally based teaching that will help you overcome these barriers to growth in Christian maturity.

The editors dedicate the *Living as a Christian* series to Christian men and women everywhere who have counted the cost and decided to follow Jesus Christ as his disciples.

Bert Ghezzi and Peter Williamson
General Editors

Introduction

LINDA WAS FURIOUS with her boss, Dr. Fenton. He had left for vacation without telling her how long he would be gone or where he could be reached in case of an emergency. During his absence, Linda began to talk behind Dr. Fenton's back. She happened to know that he wasn't getting along with his wife, and she told some of her co-workers (confidentially, of course) that divorce was imminent. When Dr. Fenton returned a week later, he caught wind of the rumors and traced them to Linda. Their relationship soured, and Linda thought it would be useless to air her grievance or apologize for speaking behind his back. After two months of increasing tension, she quit.

Jim forgot again. He had promised the O'Connors a ride to church since their car was in for repairs, and for the second time in a row, he didn't think of them until the service was half over. "It's been a busy week," he reasoned to himself, "and I just don't have a good mind for details. They are probably glad for the extra time at home anyway." Jim was surprised to see the O'Connors on his way out of church. He awkwardly expressed his relief that they had found another ride, and mumbled something about how hard it is to remember things on Sunday morning.

Since then, Jim has done his best to avoid the O'Connors.

Matt was seventeen years old and should have known better, but his younger sister *had* left her diary on the living room table, and he figured it might be good for a few innocent laughs. He picked the little diary lock and read a few pages before his sister unexpectedly walked into the room. Bursting into tears, she grabbed the diary out of his hands and stormed into her bedroom. Even though he called out after her, "What's the big deal? You were the one who left it lying around!" he felt like a louse. Gradually Matt and his sister are beginning to communicate again.

These examples illustrate a common cause of trouble in personal relationships: doing something wrong. From time to time, we simply make a mess of things. We do something which hurts someone else and damages our relationship with them. With roughly equal frequency, we find ourselves wronged by others.

This is not to say that all the problems we encounter in our relationships with others can be traced to wrongdoing. An American friend of mine, returning from three years in Indonesia, explained how she had offended an Indonesian taxi driver with her left hand. She didn't realize that in his culture the left hand was reserved for a few "dirty" jobs. To pay the cab driver with her left hand was an insult. Many of the problems we have with other people are the result of mis-understandings—whether simple ones like this, or more complex and subtle ones. But as important as clear communication is to good relationships, communication problems alone do not account for all the problems between people. If we are honest with ourselves, we have to admit that our wrongdoing—either combined with or quite apart from misunderstandings—has been an important factor in our personal relationships. Sometimes the results are serious—ruined friendships, broken marriages, parents and children at odds with each other, even the dissolution of whole Christian groups. Wherever it occurs, wrongdoing leaves a residue of bitterness, guilt, resentment, and estrangement. How should a Christian handle it?

Many of us have tried to handle our wrongdoing in the following ways:

1. Avoid the person wronged.
2. Pretend it didn't happen.
3. Try to be extra nice.
4. Hope they didn't notice.

While these approaches seem appealing at the time, we know from experience that the results are unimpressive. They simply don't repair the effects of the wrong that was done. Guilt, bitterness, and the other fruit of unrighteousness are at best covered over.

The Christian way of handling wrongdoing actually *repairs* wrongdoing; what is broken by our wrong actions and attitudes can be fixed. This happens through a process of *repentance and reconciliation*.

Of course, we've all heard about repentance and

reconciliation. We know that we must turn away from our sins and that God will forgive us; we know that we can be reconciled to God and to one another. But we tend to think of repentance and reconciliation as somewhat vague, though important, religious themes, instead of practical tools for repairing the wrongdoing that occurs in our relationships with one another.

Repentance and reconciliation are tools to be used by Christians to repair their wrongdoing, and, like any useful tool, they do the job for which they were designed. That is, they work. Unfortunately, many Christians don't use them for this purpose, and repentance and reconciliation remain only vague concepts applied in a vague manner. But waving a hammer over a nail will not drive it into the wood. To repair the damage caused by wrongdoing, we need to learn how to use the tools that God has given us.

You might think of this book as a manual for "wrongdoing repair." The first four chapters will describe the repair process step by step. Later chapters will provide more specific instruction for applying these steps in different settings.

Wrongdoing: What Is It?

Before we discuss wrongdoing repair, we should first be certain that we understand what wrongdoing is. Recent trends have produced considerable confusion about the nature of wrongdoing, and these developments have only compounded some "old-fashioned" misunderstandings about it. It will be necessary to sort through both of these sources of confusion to arrive at an accurate understanding of wrongdoing.

I am using the term "wrongdoing" as a specific subset of the larger problem of sin. The sin problem began with man's rebellion against God and God's way of doing things. The Bible understands this rebellion as the beginning of the world's woes. Widespread injustice, poverty, war, human suffering—all have their roots in man's rebellion. Sin is especially serious because it is also a *condition*, a form of spiritual bondage. It is therefore something we must be delivered from, as a slave is delivered from a cruel master.

Wrongdoing—our present concern—refers more specifically to one expression of the sin problem: our actions and attitudes which are not in accord with God's expressed will. Wrongdoing can be serious (murder, adultery, and so on) or minor (Matt's invasion of his sister's privacy), but it all stems from the same source.

Contemporary Confusion

I worked in a mental health clinic where many of the therapists had clients who were involved in serious wrongdoing. Most of the therapists, however, didn't view the idea of wrongdoing as a useful therapeutic concept, because, from their perspective, wrongdoing was *subjectively determined and relative*. We have all heard people say, "I can't tell you whether something is right or wrong. You have to decide that for yourself.

Besides, what's wrong for me may not be wrong for you." Statements like these are not based on the fact that God exists and is concerned with right and wrong—that in fact it is he who *determines* what is right and wrong. Wrongdoing is not subjectively determined. A thing is not wrong because *I* think it's wrong. It is wrong if *God* thinks it's wrong. Neither is wrongdoing relative. A thing is not wrong simply because most people agree that it's wrong. It is wrong only if God thinks it's wrong.

Many people have the impression that right and wrong are based on a fluid, ever-changing standard. Naturally, this makes it difficult to pin down wrongdoing. But this is not the Christian view. God has provided a reliable, objective standard by which we can determine whether something is right or wrong, and he has revealed it to us. Furthermore, since it is God's standard, we are not free to change it. We can cut through much of the contemporary confusion about wrongdoing if we remember that God's standards are objective, reliable, and knowable.

Old-Fashioned Confusion

Interestingly enough, this same understanding of the nature of wrongdoing can help us weed out many old-fashioned misconceptions about wrongdoing. These misconceptions, which confuse temptation, certain emotions, and mistakes with wrongdoing, are still with us.

Temptations. It is little wonder that we confuse a temptation to sin with sin itself; nearly every sin, after all, is preceded by a temptation. But experiencing a temptation to do something wrong is not the same as doing something wrong. Jesus, we know, was sinless; yet he was tempted in every way that we are. It was because Jesus never gave in to temptation that he remained sinless. We certainly don't want to seek temptation, but once it is upon us, we shouldn't think that we are guilty just because we are being tempted. If you are tempted to steal something and you resist the temptation, you may feel a bit guilty—a natural response to the fact that wrongdoing was close at hand—but in fact you are not guilty.

Emotions. There are some emotions which for one reason or another are frequently confused with wrongdoing. Anger is one of them. Some people are taught that it is wrong to feel angry. While it is true that we often commit wrongdoing when we are angry, feeling angry is not in itself wrongdoing. In some cases we may be angry unjustifiably, but as long as we don't nurse the anger along or do something wrong because we're angry, we've not committed wrongdoing. In other cases, it's right to be angry—for instance, when we see opposition to God's plan. Anger can actually motivate us to do the right thing.[1]

Mistakes. Neither are mere mistakes to be confused with wrongdoing. My daughter is learning to read and write, and, at this point, her spelling is imperfect. Most of her stories begin, "Wunz apon a tim." If her mistakes were sin, she would be in a terrible state.

Yet sometimes we relate to our mistakes as if they were instances of wrongdoing. When we make a mistake, rather than simply being disappointed or correcting it, we may feel guilty or ashamed. Unless we learn to distinguish between mistakes and wrongdoing, we will carry with us an unnecessary load of guilt.

We have opportunity enough to repair the wrong we've done without repairing the wrong we haven't done.

ONE

Admit It!

WHEN I DO SOMETHING WRONG, I hate to admit it. A few days ago, I drove to a local bookstore to pick up some books. Since my wife needed the car at 1:30 for a doctor's appointment, I set my wristwatch alarm for 1:20—just enough time for the return trip. The alarm sounded as I was browsing through an especially interesting section of books. You must realize that browsing in bookstores is one of my favorite pastimes; stepping into a bookstore is for me like entering a zone of timelessness, a kind of heavenly fog. At any rate, when the alarm sounded, I turned it off and thought that I really ought to be going. Fifteen minutes later I pulled myself away and went to pay for the books I'd selected. As is so often the case when you are in a hurry, the lady at the cash register seemed to be moving in slow motion; I think she was new at the job. After what seemed like an interminable delay, I left the store and drove home, thinking these thoughts:

"If it hadn't been for the slow saleslady, I wouldn't be so late."

"Nancy should realize that when I get into a

bookstore I lose track of time."
"Doctors are usually late for their appointments anyway."
"Americans are too fastidious about time; it's just a form of cultural bondage."

Of course it's easy to see that I was having trouble "fessing up." I knew that my wife needed the car for her appointment, but I allowed myself to indulge my desire to browse, not unaware that this would make her late. Admitting wrongdoing is the obvious first step, but it is not the easiest.

Excuses, Excuses

An outside observer of the human race might well conclude that mankind's creative instincts are most active, not in the arts or technology, but in excuse-making. While some of our most creative excuses are obviously incredible, most of them contain at least a kernel of truth—and that is precisely the problem. Because they seem at least partially true, it is easy for us to be distracted by them. Instead of proceeding to the heart of the matter—admitting and repairing our wrongdoing— we tend to look for factors that would excuse it.

"But My Intentions Were Good!" How often we excuse wrongdoing with the thought "I didn't really mean it!" Certainly there are occasions when our intentions determine whether or not a given action is wrong. For example, if I struck your jaw with the intention of breaking it, I have probably wronged you. If, on the other hand, I hit your jaw while reaching for something else, I would merely ask to be excused for my clumsiness.

More times than not, however, our intentions are beside the point. We often wrong others without specifically intending to harm them, yet our behavior is no less wrong. The wife who snaps at her husband because the children have been on her nerves all day doesn't usually mean to vent her frustrations on him. While the circumstances of the day make her behavior more understandable, they don't necessarily excuse her. If she is preoccupied with the question "Did I really mean to snap at him?" without asking the more important one, "Was it wrong for me to snap at him?" her wrongdoing is not likely to be repaired.

"I'm Not Responsible." When a person commits murder and claims insanity, his defense attorney tries to demonstrate that he is not really to blame, even though he committed the crime. The court allows for this possibility because it recognizes that in some cases a severe psychological disorder may excuse a person who has committed a crime.

In recent years the possibilities for excusing our behavior on the basis of some deeply rooted emotional problem have increased markedly. Because we are more aware of these factors than people were in ages past, we naturally tend to appeal to them in our effort to excuse our wrongdoing. We are increasingly inclined to ask,

"What made me do that?" when faced with our wrongdoing. Sometimes this helps us to understand our behavior better, enabling us to avoid it in the future, but often it simply provides fodder for our excuse-maker. There is less refuge than we think in the supposition that our stinginess can be traced to our mother's overly demanding toilet-training technique, or that our irritability is but the inevitable result of an unresolved birth trauma. Christians shouldn't avoid dealing with their wrongdoing in a Christian way just because they have some insight into its psychological causes.

"He's More to Blame than I Am." You find yourself in another heated discussion with so-and-so, that co-worker who consistently shirks his responsibility, which in turn increases your work load. As tempers flare, you make a few unfair judgments and accusations, which you later regret. You defend yourself against your troubled conscience with the thought "I know that was a low blow, but he drove me to it! Perhaps I did say some things I shouldn't have, but he's more wrong than I am!" It's a shabby defense.

Perhaps your co-worker *is* more to blame than you are. His irresponsibility may indeed be more serious than your "slips of the tongue." It is all beside the point. His wrongdoing doesn't absolve yours. His greater culpability shouldn't keep you from asking yourself, "Did I do something wrong that I ought to repair?" Jesus said, "Before you remove the splinter from your brother's eye, remove the log from your own." Even if we think the splinter is in our eye and the log is in our brother's eye, we do well to take care of our own problem first.

Euphemisms, Euphemisms. The excuse mentality is also expressed through the use of euphemisms, which Webster's dictionary defines as "the substitution of an agreeable or inoffensive expression for one that may offend or suggest something unpleasant." I keep a newspaper article which contains quotes from people describing their automobile accidents to the police, gathered from actual police reports. The quotes are rich in euphemisms.

—"A pedestrian hit me and went under my car."

—"I thought I could squeeze between two trucks when my car became squashed."

—"I had been learning to drive with power steering. I turned the wheel to what I thought was enough and found myself in a different direction going the opposite way."

—"I had been shopping for plants all day and was on my way home. As I reached an intersection a hedge sprang up obscuring my vision. I did not see the other car."

—"As I approached the intersection, a stop sign suddenly appeared in a place where no stop sign had ever appeared before. I was unable to stop in time to avoid the accident."

—"My car was legally parked as it backed into the other vehicle."[2]

The effect of this kind of language is to divert one's attention from the speaker's fault. We can resort to the same technique when admitting our own wrongdoing with statements like:

—"My earlier statements about my age were less than accurate."
—"I wasn't as loving as I could have been when I insulted her like that."
—"Talking behind his back was a mistake on my part."
—"Anger overtook me and I made contact with his jaw."

When we admit wrongdoing, we should call a spade a spade, not an agricultural implement.

Personal Responsibility:
The Christian Alternative to "Excuse Me"

In order to admit and repair the wrong we do, we must realize that we are personally responsible for it. We should be able to say, "I did it; I am responsible for it." In the Garden of Eden, Adam's *second* mistake was his failure to take responsibility for his first mistake, eating the forbidden fruit. When the Lord confronted Adam with his disobedience, Adam pointed to the Woman and said, "She made me do it!" Following his lead, Adam's wife took the same approach, saying, "That serpent over there, he made me do it!" It was the beginning of a long tradition.

Of course, Adam and Eve's efforts to shirk

responsibility were futile. In spite of their protests, God held them responsible for their actions, pronouncing curses appropriate to each of them for their wrongdoing. *All men*—not just those who haven't been clever enough to think up excuses—must give account to God for their deeds. Ultimately, we can't choose whether or not to be responsible. We *are* responsible, whether we know it or not and whether or not we like it. If we accept the fact of our personal responsibility, we will be able to repair the wrong we've done; if not, our wrongdoing will remain.

In Psalm 32 King David takes responsibility for his treacherous double-crime (committing adultery with Bathsheba and murdering her husband).

When I kept silent about my sin, my body
    wasted away,
Through my groaning all day long.
For day and night Thy hand was heavy upon
    me;
My vitality was drained away as with the fever-
    heat of summer.

I acknowledged my sin to Thee,
And my iniquity I did not hide;
I said, "I will confess my transgression to the
    Lord";
And Thou didst forgive the guilt of my sin.
                       (Ps 32:3-5)

At first David refused to accept his responsibility, and things did not go well for him.

Unrepaired, his wrongdoing came back to haunt him. It wasn't until he accepted responsibility for his actions, admitting that he had sinned, that he came to terms with God.

Most of our wrongdoing is not in this league. If we indulge in a bit of gossip, we wouldn't expect to experience David's distress. The wording of Psalm 32 or any of the other penitential psalms would be an overstatement. But the principle of personal responsibility remains in effect, regardless of the seriousness of our wrongdoing. We are just as responsible for the small things we do wrong as for the big things.

By acknowledging responsibility for our actions, we can counteract the inevitable tendency to grasp onto excuses. Were my intentions partly good? They may be; but nevertheless, I am responsible for what I do. Was I under the influence of complicated, unconscious, deeply rooted psychological defects in my personality structure? Could be, but I am still responsible for my behavior. If I've done something wrong, it's up to me to straighten it out. Is someone else to blame? If so, he is responsible for his part and I for mine.

It Takes Humility

Have you ever done something so inexcusable that your efforts at shirking responsibility seemed ridiculous, yet you just couldn't bring yourself to the point of directly admitting your wrongdoing? You were probably bumping into the age-old problem of pride.

Pride provides a raw resistance to admitting guilt. Often it will cloak itself in the guise of rationality. But it is content to prevent us from admitting the truth on any grounds. When we say, "I hate to admit it, but . . . ," we are acknowledging that we had to overcome pride in order to admit that we were wrong. The attribute that allows us to overcome our pride is humility. Without it, pride will be unrestrained in its effort to keep us from admitting our wrongdoing.

Sometimes we think that pride can only be tamed by practicing a kind of groveling humility that says, "I know that I'm a jerk—always blowing it. If there is any possibility that I've done something wrong, I probably have." But that's not genuine humility. Genuine humility is based on an accurate self-assessment. In his letter to the Romans, Paul wrote, "Do not think of yourself more highly than you ought, but rather think of yourself with sober judgment" (Rom 12:3). The ideal that Paul presents is a *sober* assessment of ourselves. That means viewing ourselves as we are—not exaggerating our strengths or our faults. We don't become humble by exaggerating our faults. If we view ourselves with sober judgment, we will readily recognize that we are capable of wrongdoing. While we will be displeased by our sin, we won't be so surprised by it that we cannot allow ourselves to admit it.

Even though Jesus never sinned, he still provides us with a model of humility which can inspire us to overcome pride in admitting our wrongdoing. Jesus manifested humility by taking the lowly position of a servant: "Although He existed in the form of God, [He] did not regard equality with God a thing to be grasped, but emptied Himself, taking the form of a bond-servant, and being made in the likeness of men. . . . He humbled Himself by becoming obedient to the point of death" (Phil 2:6-8).

When we admit wrongdoing, either to the Lord or to the person we've wronged, we are assuming a position of lowliness. To go to a friend and say, "Look, I was wrong when I talked to you the way I did the other day," is literally a humbling experience. It is the kind of experience that pride resists tooth and nail, but which Christlike humility urges us to embrace.

TWO

Renounce It!

ONCE AN OLD CAR of mine was leaking badly, so a friend and I went out to see what was wrong. We poked around for quite a while until we finally diagnosed the problem: a broken water pump. For the next ten minutes we looked at the pump, saying things like, "Yep, looks like that old water pump has had it, wouldn't you say so?"

"Right you are. Just look at that water dripping out." After a while we looked at each other and laughed. It was obvious that neither of us wanted to start fixing it. Instead we were content to dwell on the diagnosis.

Admitting our wrongdoing is the diagnosis. Inasmuch as the diagnosis leads to treatment, it is the first step in the restorative process; but unless it is followed by specific action, it is merely an academic exercise.

Once we've taken the difficult step of admitting our wrongdoing, we ought to specifically renounce it. To renounce something is to decide that we don't want any part of it. At its root, renunciation is not a feeling, an inclination, or an internal disposition; it is a decision. We *decide* to renounce our wrongdoing.

A decision is needed because we are often very attached to our wrongdoing. Renouncing a particular wrong attitude or action may be the last thing we want to do.

I've counselled a number of young single Christians who have become entangled in romantic relationships that have involved sexual behavior appropriate only to marriage. After reviewing the Christian teaching, most agree that their behavior is wrong. But many also experience a strong inner resistance to changing the situation. Naturally! Sex is enjoyable. It's not easy to renounce wrongdoing which is so fun and seems so rewarding. A person in this situation can know that a particular action is wrong, openly admit it, and still not make a single move to change. What's missing? Renunciation—a decision to give up wrongdoing in spite of contrary inclinations.

I remember vividly an occasion when I had tremendous difficulty renouncing wrongdoing even though I had admitted that I was in the wrong. I used to be unusually critical of other Christians. Before becoming a member of the Christian community to which I now belong, I met with one of the leaders to tell him everything I didn't like about the group. In retrospect, I realize that some of my criticisms were fair, while others were not. But even if my criticisms were legitimate, my attitude was off. Fortunately, the man I was meeting with had the courage to tell me just that. He said, "Ken, you're coming into this with a critical spirit, and that is the wrong way for you to relate to brothers and sisters in Christ. I don't think you're going to be in a position to help us improve unless you give up this attitude."

I had no problem admitting it; I knew I was too critical of others. In fact, I secretly prided myself on being critical. But when he addressed me so pointedly, I realized for the first time that the Lord wanted me to renounce my critical attitude. I received his correction graciously, even thanking him for his honesty, but as I drove home from the meeting, I went through a fierce internal struggle. I was beyond trying to justify my attitude; I just didn't want to give it up! Eventually I did decide to part with it. So I prayed, "Lord, I don't want to hold on to my critical spirit. I know it is wrong and I renounce it! I don't want any part of it!" For years I had recognized that I was too critical of others, but nothing changed until I took that important step.

Effective Renunciation

Verbalize it. Often we recognize a pattern of wrongdoing and merely think to ourselves, "I really ought to stop that." But as a mere thought it is like a puff of smoke in a windstorm. A spoken statement is much more concrete, and therefore more effective.

State it decisively. "I suppose I shouldn't be so critical of others" is not a decisive statement. If we are indecisive because we are not sure that something is actually wrong, we should consider the matter further until it is clear one way or the other. Asking a trusted friend's opinion can help clarify whether a particular attitude or action is wrong. But once we realize that something *is* wrong, an indecisive statement of renunciation carries within it the seed of evasion.

Be specific. "I really blew it that time, and I'm going to stop that business" is a start. But how did you blow it? What was the occasion? And precisely what do you want to avoid in the future? When we renounce something, we should be as specific as possible so that it is clear just what we are renouncing.

Be vigorous. When I was struggling with my critical attitude, I knew that I would have to renounce it vigorously if I were to renounce it at all. A meekly stated "I'm going to stop this critical attitude" just wouldn't have been enough. When I am convinced that the Lord wants me to repent of an attitude or action that is difficult for me to turn from, I have gone so far as to quickly insure privacy, and then state my renunciation to the Lord in no uncertain terms—loudly and sometimes repeatedly.

We can thoroughly undermine renunciation if we don't also take whatever steps will help us to avoid repeating the wrongdoing in the future. The traditional and wise advice to "avoid the near occasion of sin" is one such step, but there are others.

Don't Give Up!

We might think of sin as a host of door-to-door salesmen from the enemy camp. Some of the salesmen are timid. If one knocks at the door, we let him into the front hallway, then boot him out as soon as we realize what he is trying to sell. This type may never return. But other of the merchants of unrighteousness are more shrewd and persistent (or their wares may be more appealing to us). If one of these characters knocks at the door, he is likely to step uninvited into the front hallway, and we may be foolish enough to ask him into the living room for a cup of coffee. We may even sign up for some of his merchandise before we come to our senses, jump to our feet and say, "The deal's off. You're a phoney! Now get out of my house!" But having achieved a measure of success, he will probably return. If, through a combination of our own weakness and the salesman's persistence, we find ourselves entertaining him again, we must be prepared to boot him out—again and again and again, until we have slammed the door in his face for the last time.

When confronting deeply rooted, recurrent patterns of wrongdoing we may be tempted to think: "Ah, what's the use of renouncing this? I know it won't be the last time I do it, no matter how vigorously I renounce it now." Renunciation is not a guaranteed quick fix, especially if the wrongdoing has become a habit. Without thinking that committing the wrong again is inevitable, we should set ourselves to renounce it whenever it recurs. We should renounce it with the intention of never committing it again. But if we do, we should renounce it again.

Renouncing Hand and Foot

Never one to mince his words, Jesus said, "If your hand or foot causes you to stumble, cut it off and throw it from you; it is better for you to enter life crippled or lame, than having two hands or two feet, to be cast into the eternal fire. And if your eye causes you to stumble, pluck it out, and throw it from you. It is better for you to enter life with one eye, than having two eyes, to be cast into the hell of fire" (Mt 18:8-9). This is not a teaching about self-mutilation; the early disciples did not go about lopping off hands and feet. But it is a teaching about renouncing wrongdoing, and a very strong teaching indeed. Jesus' point is this: wrongdoing is so serious that when it occurs *we must do whatever is necessary to renounce it.*

This summer I was walking through a section of a university campus, where there were several young women who seemed to have forgotten much of their clothing. I realized that I was in for a struggle with sexual temptation unless I took quick action. Thanking the Lord for my rather severe nearsightedness, I merely took off my glasses—a handy and painless way to "pluck out the eye" while retaining the option of putting it back later. This may seem like an extreme example, unless you've been on a university campus recently.

Renouncing wrongdoing can sometimes be painless—as easy as slipping off a pair of glasses. But more often it is painful: and the teaching of Jesus is that even when it is painful it must be done. Consider, for example, the predicament of a wife whose husband has been neglecting her. She falls in love with another man and, before she knows it, finds herself embroiled in an adulterous affair. Though she knows that adultery is forbidden, she also knows that she hasn't felt better in years. In her mind the relationship is "meaningful," "committed," even "life-giving." To end such a relationship would seem like cutting off a hand. It would be painful. It would seem to involve a profound injury to oneself. It would certainly be accompanied by a deep sense of loss. But the relationship is wrong—a stumbling block in the way of obedience to God. It must be renounced. The hand must be cut off, the eye plucked out. The same is true of any other stumbling block, any other sin that clings to us: we must take whatever action is necessary to renounce it.

Renunciation: Godly Grief, Not Self-Condemnation

Sorrow for wrongdoing should normally accompany renunciation. By "sorrow" I don't mean self-condemnation. Authentic sorrow for wrong-

doing is focused on the person injured and on the
Lord, who has been disobeyed. Authentic sorrow
leads to a deep resolution to repair the damage and
avoid further wrongdoing. In other words, sorrow
for sin helps us to repent and to make a clear break
with sin.

Once I was with a group of men relaxing after a
good meal. We began to sing some Christian songs
with great enthusiasm, but after a few songs, our
singing took on a form of mockery as we made fun
of certain Christian songs that didn't suit our
tastes. Afterwards, I realized that this wasn't
right; it wasn't respectful of other Christians, and
it wasn't respectful of the Lord, whose name was
being dishonored by the way we sang. Though on
the surface it didn't seem like a terrible thing, I
experienced a sense of grief for having participated
in it. Then and there I resolved not to do it again
and spoke with the other men about it.

Self-condemnation, on the other hand, does not
usually lead to effective repentance. It is focused
on the self, not on the person wronged or on the
Lord. Self-condemnation leads to despair, self-
hatred, and self-pity. As Christians have lost the
ability to recognize wrongdoing, repent of it, and
be reconciled, they have come increasingly under
the tyranny of self-condemnation, at times even
confusing it with a type of Christian piety. But the
voice of self-condemnation is essentially deceptive:
"You've done it again! How can you even call
yourself a Christian? God is sick and tired of you
and your sinful ways." Christians who experience

regular self-condemnation are not being pious; they are suffering from an emotional or spiritual problem. They need to be freed from this problem, not encouraged.[3]

Paul distinguishes between godly grief and this form of false sorrow in his second letter to the Corinthians, which followed upon a previous letter calling them to repent of certain practices: "For though I caused you sorrow by my letter, I do not regret it; though I did regret it—for I see that that letter caused you sorrow, though only for a while—I now rejoice, not that you were made sorrowful, but that you were made sorrowful to the point of repentance; for you were made sorrowful according to the will of God, in order that you might not suffer loss in anything through us. For the sorrow that is according to the will of God produces a repentance without regret, leading to salvation; but the sorrow of the world produces death. For behold what earnestness this very thing, this godly sorrow, has produced in you: what vindication of yourselves, what indignation, what fear, what longing, what zeal, what avenging of wrong! (2 Cor 7:8-11).

The contrast between godly sorrow and self-condemnation is vividly illustrated in the responses of Peter and Judas, both of whom had denied the Lord before his death. After Judas betrayed Jesus, Matthew's Gospel reports that he "felt remorse and returned the thirty pieces of silver to the chief priests and elders. . . . and he went away and hanged himself" (Mt 27:3, 5).

Judas's sorrow literally led to death. Peter, on the other hand, also experienced sorrow over his denial of the Lord, as Matthew again records: "And he went out and wept bitterly" (Mt 26:75). Yet Peter's grief led to repentance and reconciliation with the Lord and the other disciples. Because it was godly grief, it led to life, to a clean slate, to freedom from guilt.

THREE

Be Reconciled

BY ADMITTING AND RENOUNCING wrongdoing, a person completes the act of repentance. The repair work, however, has not been completed until the damage done to the relationship—with the Lord or with others—has been repaired. Steps one and two can usually be taken by oneself. Step three necessarily involves the person wronged.

After someone has repented of wrongdoing, they must then be reconciled with the injured party. Specifically, they should go to the person wronged, confess the wrong, and ask for forgiveness from the other person.

First, Go to Him

Jesus said, "If therefore you are presenting your offering at the altar, and there remember that your brother has something against you, leave your offering before the altar and *go*; first be reconciled to your brother, and then come and present your offering" (Mt 5:23-24). To be reconciled we must first do what Jesus said to do: We must go to the person wronged. This command to "go" can be one of the most difficult to obey. Going to a person we've wronged to be reconciled is not one of our favorite activities, and we aren't beyond looking for ways to avoid it.

"Aren't there any exceptions?" Yes, but not many. When the person you've wronged is no longer alive or otherwise absolutely unavailable, there's obviously not much you can do except seek God's forgiveness and leave the rest in his hands. There may also be occasions when going to the person you've wronged would only make matters worse, but these are rare.

"But it doesn't seem to bother him much." Just because the person you've wronged isn't hopping mad about it doesn't mean that you should sweep the matter under the rug. Your relationship may seem undisturbed. But what appears to be going on with that person is beside the point. Most people know when they've been wronged and some react more than others. Yet even if they don't, the effects of wrongdoing— resentment, anger, and so on—can work well below the surface. I remember feeling a bit cool toward a person, without being able to put my finger on the cause. Then he came to me and repented for a few things he had said. It wasn't until then that I realized I had been wronged; after I forgave him, we got along much better.

"Would a letter or a phone call do?" Usually the most direct and personal way is the best way. A face-to-face meeting. Of course, sometimes prac-

tical factors prevent this, and there are special situations when a phone call or a note of apology might be better. But lack of courage should not be the grounds for one of these approaches.

"Yes, but I get embarrassed when I do things like that." It *can* be embarrassing to go to a person to be reconciled, though it is often not nearly as embarrassing as one might anticipate. Even so, there are no known cases of sudden death due to embarrassment, even in its most acute form. As my father used to wisely advise me from time to time: "Tough. Do it anyway."

Second, Confess to Him

Having approached the person we've wronged, we ought to admit our wrongdoing. "I was the source of those rumors that have been circulating about you. I was wrong to have started them."

When the prodigal son realized that he had wronged his father by squandering his inheritance, he first went to his father and confessed his wrongdoing: "Father, I have sinned against heaven and against you." He didn't say, "Listen, Dad, I know there have been some bad feelings between us, but let's put that behind us now." He knew his wrongdoing had caused the broken relationship and that an acknowledgment of this fact—a confession to his father—was required.

Here it must be noted that we shouldn't confess to someone simply because we harbor some negative feelings toward them.

"Denise, there's something I feel I ought to share with you."

"What's that?"

"Well, to be honest with you, I've been feeling bad about you ever since we met."

"Gee, have I done something wrong?"

"Oh no, not at all."

"Then what is it?"

"I'm ashamed to say it, but for some reason the way you laugh just irks me. There's probably nothing you can do about it, but I thought I owed you a confession. I feel much better now."

"I'm so glad."

Get to the Point. Avoid the tendency to hem, haw, and beat around the bush. Few things are as unnerving as waiting for someone to get to the point.

"Say Ken." (pause)

"Yes?"

"I've been thinking." (pause)

"Uh-huh?"

"Well, it's just that I noticed that sometimes when I find myself in certain situations, I have this certain tendency to, well, you know. (pause)

"I'm not sure that I do."

"I don't suppose you would . . . Well anyway it was like I was saying . . . "

When I acknowledge my wrongdoing to the person I've wronged, I try to formulate what I want to say beforehand so that I can get to the point as quickly and painlessly as possible.

Don't Exaggerate. If you have a tender conscience, watch out for exaggerated confessions.

"Jenny, I feel just awful about what I did to you the other day."

"Oh, what was that?"

"I forgot to pick you up like I promised. I know it was a terribly irresponsible thing to do, and frankly, I don't know what got into me; I'll never forgive myself."

Unless the wrongdoing is objectively serious, avoid terms like "terrible," "awful," and "reprehensible."

Many people have trouble with inappropriate guilt feelings; if you are one of these, your feelings won't be a reliable guide for talking with the other person.

Don't Be Flippant. At the same time, we shouldn't speak lightly of anything we are confessing, no matter how small.

"Joe, I shouldn't have made fun of your nose the other day, though you've got to admit, I could hardly help it. Seriously, I should watch out for that."

"Thanks a lot."

Our culture tends to project a light, casual, even flippant attitude towards wrongdoing, as well as to place a high value on quick-witted, lighthearted, and at times flippant speech. We sometimes imitate these patterns unknowingly or simply fall back on them when we are nervous or insecure about what we are doing. Making light of our wrongdoing, however, does not express an attitude of genuine repentance. Our tone of voice and choice of words should express our sincerity.

Third, Seek Forgiveness

The Christian approach to reconciliation is based on the fact that forgiveness exists and that forgiveness actually takes away sin. In the economic realm, forgiveness refers to a particular financial transaction—cancelling a debt. I borrowed money from the United States government to help cover my college expenses. The loan had a "forgiveness clause," which allowed part of the debt to be cancelled for each year that I worked in the field for which I had been trained. If I should die before the loan is paid off, the remaining portion would also be cancelled. In reference to wrongdoing, forgiveness is like cancelling a debt. To forgive someone is to decide to relate to them as if the wrong never happened. When we ask for forgiveness, we are asking people we've wronged to cancel our debt—to relate to us as if the wrong never happened. When they forgive us, they put that cancellation into effect. They say, "I'm going to relate to you as if it never happened."

This capacity to forgive is not something we acquire out of the blue; it is derived from God's capacity to forgive. Because it is God's nature to forgive, those who share in God's nature share this same capacity to forgive. Those who don't know the God who forgives and who have not experienced being forgiven for their wrongdoing may well have a very limited capacity to forgive others. They may be forced to find other ways of dealing with wrongdoing. But the Christian knows that through forgiveness wrongdoing can be removed—not just covered over, but actually taken away.

When you ask for forgiveness, be explicit. Say, "Will you forgive me?" While this sounds simple enough, most Christians don't do it this way. Even when people go to the trouble of trying to be reconciled directly, the issue of forgiveness is rarely handled in a direct way. Instead, forgiveness is assumed, glossed over, forgotten, or bypassed.

The normal manner of expressing regret—"I'm sorry" followed by "That's OK"—is not enough to accomplish true reconciliation. The "I'm sorry/That's OK" method is appropriate when forgiveness is not needed—when someone merely makes a mistake, for example—but it does not deal effectively with wrongdoing. "I'm sorry" expresses regret, and nothing more. It says nothing about personal responsibility, the wrongness of the action, or the need to be forgiven. All these issues are cloaked in ambiguity. "That's OK" is equally vague; it implies that "what you did wasn't such a bad thing to do. So let's forget about it." But wrongdoing is *not* OK. The injury is real, and the injured party is not likely to forget it. To cut through this ambiguity, we should be explicit: "I have done this wrong, and I don't want to repeat it. Will you forgive me?" By asking directly, we allow the other person an opportunity for a specific response: "I forgive you." The words may differ, but they should include a clear order of reconciliation: an acknowledgment of wrongdoing, the resolution to change, and the gift of forgiveness.

Forgiving

While it is important to seek forgiveness when you've done something wrong, it is even more important to give forgiveness when you are the person wronged. Jesus left no room for doubt about this: "If your brother sins, rebuke him, and if he repents, forgive him; and if he sins against you seven times in the day, and turns to you seven times, and says, 'I repent,' you must forgive him" (Lk 17:3-4). In this passage the Lord describes the responsibility of the offender to go to the person wronged and repent to him; yet he is even more elaborate in his description of the responsibility of the person wronged.

Go to the Offender. Often we go to everyone *but* the person who wronged us. A friend of mine who teaches in a prison was having trouble with one of his co-workers, who had a reputation for being belligerent. He brought up the difficulty with his boss, who gave him this advice: "What you have to do with her, Dan, is discuss your situation with a group of other people. Win them over to your side; then you'll outnumber her." Dan didn't take his boss' advice because he realized it didn't reflect a biblical approach to working out bad relationships. Instead, he went straight to the woman and worked the problem out with her. When we've been wronged, we have a responsibility to go to the person who has wronged us, rather than to deal indirectly with our resentment or anger.

Forgive Him. It is one thing to go raging to the person who wronged us, with the intention of "telling him off," and quite another to go with the intention of being reconciled. Jesus teaches that the intention of both parties involved should be to be reconciled—for the offender, who is seeking forgiveness, and for the offended, who is seeking to forgive.

This does not mean that we should never become angry at the offender, or that we should prematurely excuse the wrong done to us. On several occasions, Jesus taught by word and example that we may need to rebuke the person. Strong words are sometimes needed to prick a dulled conscience or bring a person to repentance. But even when strong words are called for, our *goal* in going to the person is reconciliation. We should want to forgive the offender. There have been times when I've been so angry with someone's behavior that I was almost disappointed when the person readily repented. Reconciliation was less than my primary intention.

Forgiveness is so important that we should be prepared to forgive others regardless of whether they repent. If we pray, "Forgive us our sins, as we forgive those who sin against us," then we should even be willing to forgive the person who does not seek our forgiveness.

A young married woman had spent the day at her parents' home. When her father returned from work, he was in a sour mood and began berating her husband, her mother, and herself before shutting himself in his bedroom for the evening. The next morning, this young woman was furious with her father—for good reason. But even before she went to him she had to decide, then and there, to forgive him, whether or not he apologized for what he had said. What did this act of forgiveness accomplish? Alone, it did not bring about a complete reconciliation between the woman and her father. That kind of reconciliation would occur when the father turned away from his wrongdoing and received his daughter's forgiveness. But it did allow the woman to get rid of the kind of bitterness toward her father which would have eaten away at her like a festering sore; it allowed her to relate respectfully and lovingly toward him in spite of his behavior. Because she had decided to forgive him, she was able to speak directly to him about his behavior without communicating bitterness or hatred.

Forgive and Forgive Again. Estimates of how often we should be expected to forgive another range from seven times in a day to seven times seventy (Lk 17:3-4). The point is not that when after being forgiven twice in a day, someone has five remaining chances that day and 488 in their lifetime. Jesus is teaching that reconciliation is so important that there can be no limitation to our willingness to forgive others. We are to forgive again and again.

Jesus knew how human relationships work. He knew that most often we wrong those we are in closest contact with. My wife has forgiven me more than she has forgiven any other person, not because I am such a terrible person, but because I have had so many opportunities to offend her. Most of the people who offend us have done so before. We should be prepared to forgive them as often as they need to be forgiven.

How to Forgive. Just as we ought to be direct when we ask for forgiveness, we ought to be direct when we grant it. Sometimes, out of concern for the other person, we try to minimize what another has done with a casual "Oh, don't worry about it" or "Forget it; it was nothing." We may even be embarrassed by their request to be forgiven and try to laugh it off or change the subject. None of this helps the other person. Instead we should simply say, "I forgive you." When spoken clearly and directly these simple words can bring relief to the guilty party and restoration to a damaged relationship.

Forgiveness should be granted generously, not begrudgingly. By nature, forgiveness is an act of grace, of unmerited favor. It cannot be earned; it can only be given freely. To say, "I forgive you," through clenched teeth, followed by "*this* time," is actually something less than forgiveness.

What can we do when we don't feel like forgiving someone who comes to us seeking forgiveness? First of all, we must realize that we don't have any other option. We are commanded to forgive—not by the person who wronged us, but by the Lord himself. Our willingness to forgive others is connected to our receiving God's forgiveness ("Forgive us our trespasses as we forgive those who trespass against us"). Second, forgiveness is not a feeling. If it were, we wouldn't speak of the "act of forgiveness." Forgiveness is our action toward the other person, based on a decision not to hold the wrong against them. We can choose to forgive even when our feelings are saying, "no, never!" Third, there may be occasions when our feelings are so strong that the best we can do is to tell the person, "Look, I want to forgive you, and in my heart I do, but I've still got some resentment and anger to deal with. Let's discuss it later." Once we've had time to cool down and gain some emotional distance, we can go back to the person and reaffirm our forgiveness.

Finally, Shake On It. After either giving forgiveness, or receiving it with a "thank you," it is good to express the fact that your relationship is now on a good footing again. Depending on the relationship, a handshake, a hug, or some other form of physical affection is a good way to seal the process of reconciliation. Unless there are some other matters to discuss relevant to the incident, move on to another topic of conversation. This expresses the fact that the incident is over and is no longer a matter for consideration. When the breach in the relationship is more serious, specific action to strengthen the relationship may be called for. Set up a time to have a meal together, to recreate, or just to visit. I've often found that going through the process of reconciliation actually deepens a relationship, making it even stronger than it was before the difficulty arose.

FOUR

Make Restitution

BEFORE RON WAS A CHRISTIAN, he worked for a large pharmaceutical corporation. During his years with the firm, he stole several things, ranging from office supplies to filing cabinets. When Ron committed himself to the Lord, he realized that all his rationalizations ("they won't miss it; everyone else does it; it's not like taking money from a person") couldn't hide the fact that he was guilty of stealing. Naturally he repented and asked God's forgiveness, but this didn't seem to be enough. Though he had since stopped working for the firm and moved to another city, Ron felt that his repentance would not be complete until he returned the stolen material.

When he added up all that he could remember taking from the company, the sum came to three thousand dollars, in addition to the few items he still had with him. Since Ron didn't have that much money, he spent the next few months working extra jobs to earn it.

Finally, with a check for three thousand dollars and a carload of assorted items, Ron drove to his old job to speak with his supervisor. When he explained that he wanted to return some stolen goods and pay back three thousand dollars, his former boss was flabbergasted. He was aware that employees often took things that didn't belong to them, but he had never heard of anyone admitting it, much less making an inventory of stolen goods and offering repayment. Not knowing what to do, he referred Ron to a higher level manager. The case was referred upward so many times that Ron eventually found himself in the office of a vice-president.

Ron confessed to the vice-president and asked his forgiveness as he gave him the check. The executive was so impressed with his honesty that he initially refused to accept the money. (Eventually he agreed to contribute it to a charitable organization.) The vice-president asked Ron what prompted his action. Ron told him how God had changed his perspective, and before long the vice-president of the company was expressing his own need for God's action in his life.

The final step in repairing wrongdoing is to do what Ron did—make restitution whenever possible. The law of Israel contained specific regulations for restitution: "If a man steals an ox or a sheep, and kills it or sells it, he shall pay five oxen for an ox, and four sheep for a sheep. He shall make restitution" (Ex 22:1). In the New Testament, restitution is seen as evidence of true repentance.

While passing through Jericho, Jesus noticed a small man perched in a sycamore tree. The man was the town's chief tax collector, Zacchaeus, and like other tax collectors he was rich. It was widely believed that he acquired his wealth by means of the corrupt practices common to his profession. To everyone's surprise, Jesus called Zacchaeus down from the tree and invited himself over for dinner. After talking with Jesus, the tax collector had a remarkable change of heart and said to him, "Lord, the half of my goods I give to the poor; and if I have defrauded any one of anything, I restore it fourfold" (Lk 19:8). Zacchaeus was offering to make restitution for his wrongdoing, and Jesus seemed to think that his offer marked a significant event: "Today," he said, "salvation has come to this house" (19:9). Presumably it was Zacchaeus' contact with Jesus that brought him to the point of repentance; he expressed this change of heart and his own sincerity by offering to make restitution for any wrong he had done.

Restitution is not an attempt to earn forgiveness. The idea of earned forgiveness is a contradiction of terms. Forgiveness cannot be earned; it is an act of grace which can only be given freely. Restitution is an outward sign that a person is sincere about repenting. It expresses the fact that he wants what is best for the one who has been wronged. It is part of taking responsibility for the wrong done: "Since I am responsible for this mess, I want to make it up to you if I can."

Restitution should not *replace* the other steps of the repair process. We may be tempted to think that being "extra nice" to someone we've wronged will counterbalance the wrong so that we don't have to deal with it directly. But restitution of this kind can actually be counter-productive.

On the other hand, the first three steps of wrongdoing repair can be rendered ineffective *without* restitution. Perhaps you've heard the story of a lumberyard worker who had stolen a piece of lumber from his company every day for twenty years. Finally his conscience caught up with him and he stopped taking the boards home. He even went to his pastor to confess to him. As an act of penance, the clergyman directed the lumberyard worker to build a small addition to the church. "If you've got the nails, Reverend," he replied, "I've got the lumber." His repair job was obviously incomplete.

Restitution is an obvious step when your wrongdoing has resulted in another person's material loss. This would include returning stolen goods, promptly repaying a forgotten loan, re-placing lost or damaged property, and so on. When the wrongdoing is serious, or malicious, it may be appropriate to replace more than the amount involved. But material losses are not the only damage for which restitution can be made.

Other Forms of Restitution

"How great a forest is set ablaze by a small fire!" James observed (3:5), referring to the damage unrighteous speech can do. If a person's reputation is damaged by the forest fire we set ablaze with our flaming tongue, we ought to take steps to restore it, just as we would take steps to restore any other valuable possession.

Suppose you spoke against a friend behind his back, and your comments were likely to damage his reputation. Restitution would then involve going back to the people who heard your remarks (and any people to whom they have passed them along) and attempting to restore your friend's reputation: "It was wrong of me to speak behind Jim's back like that; besides, he deserves more credit than my remarks gave him." When specific efforts to withdraw your comments are futile, restitution might still be made by speaking positively about the person in the future.

Some forms of wrongdoing can result in extra demands on another person's time. When this happens, we ought to offer to help make up for the time he or she lost. For instance, if a co-worker has had to handle one of my responsibilities because of my negligence, I could make restitution by offering to do something for them and attempting to relieve any time pressures that my wrongdoing may have created for them.

Although "being extra nice" is an inadequate strategy for handling wrongdoing, performing special favors for the person wronged is an expression of restitution that is often warranted—especially when there isn't a more specific way of making restitution. If I am impatient with my wife for a few days, it's not as if there is any concrete loss that can be identified and restored. To be sure, our relationship will suffer due to my impatience, and the primary way for me to repair things is to repent and seek my wife's forgiveness. In addition, a bouquet of flowers or a surprise dinner out of the house is a good expression of the sincerity of my repentance, as well as a salve for injured feelings.

Summary

The preceding chapters have outlined a specific, step-by-step procedure for repairing wrongdoing. The steps can be summarized as follows: First, we must *admit* our wrongdoing. To do this, we need to understand what wrongdoing is and what it isn't. We need to overcome our natural tendency to make excuses, to hide behind euphemisms, and to give in to pride. Second, we must *renounce* our wrongdoing. Renunciation involves a conscious turning away from the wrongdoing, a resolute decision never to repeat it. It may also include taking practical steps to avoid the occasion for wrongdoing. Step three involves going to the person we've wronged to *be reconciled* with him or her. In the person's presence, we should confess what we've done wrong, state our intention to repent, and ask their forgiveness. We should be straightforward: "It was wrong of me to _____ and I repent. Will you forgive me?" Finally, we should *make restitution* for any damage caused by our wrongdoing, as a way of taking responsibility for our action and attitudes, and as an expression of sincere repentance.

It is not always easy to know where and how to begin implementing this approach to repairing wrongdoing. What about wrongdoing that occurred months or years ago? How is the Christian approach applied among other Christians? In the family—between husband and wife, and among parents and children? How is it applied among people who are used to handling wrongdoing differently? The next three chapters will address these kind of questions.

FIVE

How to Begin

MY WIFE'S PARENTS were flying over the Gulf of Mexico in a commercial airliner when the plane began to shake and lurch. After a brief time of confusion, the pilot announced that one of the two jet engines had failed. They were headed for the nearest landing area, which was still thirty minutes away. The stewardess instructed the passengers in the use of life preservers in case of an emergency landing. Fortunately, the crippled plane landed safely (though it was sobering to see the runway lined with fire engines and ambulances).

During the last thirty minutes over the Gulf of Mexico many of the passengers probably considered their past lives and the people who were important to them. Imagine how unsettling it would be at a time like that to remember wrong actions that haven't been repaired or relationships that remain unreconciled.

Long-Gone Wrongs

Rather than wait for our life to "flash before our eyes" at the moment of death, we ought to take time now—when there is still time to repair wrongdoing—to soberly review our past actions and the condition of our relationships. It may save us considerable grief when we face that final life-review.

If you haven't done so already, consider taking some time to conduct a review of your past life in order to handle any unrepaired wrongdoing. This can be done with a mature, trusted Christian whose wisdom you respect, or it can be done on your own. There are several advantages to having a Christian counsellor to discuss your past with: some people think more clearly when they are speaking with someone else; a counsellor can keep you from getting too introspective, help you handle painful memories, and so on. Conducting such a review with a pastor or counsellor is not always possible or necessary; in that case, you can do it on your own.

To conduct a review of your past life, find a quiet place where you can spend an hour or two free from distractions, and take along some paper and a pencil. Open the review with a time of prayer in which you thank the Lord for forgiving your sins, and for giving you the power to follow him. State your intention to renounce all wrongdoing, past and present, and ask him to reveal any past actions which are in need of specific repentance and any relationships in need of reconciliation. Then think about your past life in some orderly way, perhaps by thinking first of your childhood years and then the years leading to the present. As specific wrong actions come to mind, write them down. (Some you may want to list individually, while others may need to be grouped together.) Don't get sidetracked with any one particular wrongdoing—just write it down and move along. Also list the significant relationships in your life which come easily to mind. Go down the list and underline the relationships that have been damaged by wrongdoing. Then think about each of these and jot down any relevant specifics.

Now go over the list you made of your past wrongdoing and repent for each item, asking for God's forgiveness. Many of the things on your list may involve some other person; in that case, plan to go to the wronged and ask for their forgiveness as well. Of course, this will not be possible, or even desirable, in every situation. For example, you may have had a disordered romantic relationship that ended on a sour note. Reestablishing contact with the other person may only complicate the situation.

You may find that a few of your close relationships are not in very good shape. Perhaps you experience longstanding tension with your father, mother, spouse, or a sibling. While you can repent immediately to the Lord for the way your actions have affected the relationship, you will probably need to develop a long-range strategy for improving the relationship. Such a strategy might include repenting to the person for specific actions, talking with them to work out misunderstandings, and taking some natural steps to build the relationship.

One young man I know made a serious Christian

commitment in his early twenties. At that time his relationship with his father was poor—the turbulence and rebellion characteristic of the late 1960s had taken its toll. The young man identified what he had done wrong during that time and repented to his father, but he knew that it would take more than a good conversation to fully repair the relationship. His father was understandably skeptical; he had seen his son go through "phases" before, and he wondered whether this "Christian thing" wasn't just another phase. While now, after a few years, father and son are basically reconciled, the relationship is still recovering from its earlier problems. The purpose of a life-review is to identify past actions and relationships that are in need of repair, to repent immediately to the Lord, and as soon as possible to other people, and to begin working toward the restoration of more seriously damaged relationships.

Another helpful step in the review process is to write down the names of people that you hold a grudge against. Some of them may have wronged you in specific ways; in some cases it might help to bring this to their attention. In any case, you can decide to unilaterally forgive them all; you might state aloud to the Lord your intention to forgive them and tear up the list as a concrete expression of that forgiveness.

A life-review is not supposed to be a long, tortuous period of introspection. It should take no longer than an hour, and it is not necessary or possible to remember every single unrepaired wrong you have done. Do not dwell on the details of your past wrongdoing or attempt to analyze the interpersonal dynamics of every relationship problem you have had. Remember, the purpose is not to wallow in guilt feelings and become depressed. The purpose is to identify wrongs that you can repent of, so that you can be free from guilt and can begin what may be a long process of improving some troubled relationships. For some, conducting the review with a trusted pastor or Christian counsellor may not only be advantageous but necessary in order to avoid unhealthy introspection, which leads to excessive guilt feelings and depression.

Whether you conduct your life-review yourself or talk these matters over with a mature Christian, it is almost always helpful to confess the wrongdoing that comes to light during the review to another Christian whom you respect and trust. James, when giving advice about praying for those who are sick, said, "Confess your sins to one another" (Jas 5:16). Combining a life-review with a general confession to another trusted Christian can help you make a clear break with past wrongdoing.

When we confess our sins to the Lord and one another we should remember the promise found in the first letter of John: "If we confess our sins, He is faithful and righteous to forgive us our sins and to cleanse us from all unrighteousness" (1 Jn 1:9).

Finally, you may want to set aside a day for

fasting and prayer to accompany the life-review. The Israelites did this on the Day of Atonement (Yom Kippur), a national day of repentance on which they were told to "humble their souls" (Lv 16:29)—a reference to fasting. Fasting is an expression of mourning and by doing it we express the godly grief that ought to accompany repentance.

Thereafter

If you've been a Christian for a while, you won't be naive enough to think that you will be able to avoid all wrongdoing between now and the end of your life. But there is no reason why you can't repair the wrongs you do commit. Rather than allow unrepaired wrongdoing to accumulate, resolve to repair it as soon as you become aware of it. And don't let the size or seriousness of the wrong deter you; if it's wrong, it should be repaired.

Repairing wrongdoing doesn't always have to be a "big deal"—an experience requiring a lot of time and emotional energy. Not all of our repentance will be as intense as David's after he killed Bathsheba's husband or the prodigal son's after he broke his relationship with his father. Many of the things we will repent of will be less serious than these. Repairing wrongdoing should never become casual—on the order of "excuse me"—but neither does it have to be a crisis experience.

On the other hand, if we've never actually said to someone, "I was wrong and I repent. Will you forgive me?" we may find that it does indeed seem like a "big deal" until we've had some practice. I can't even remember what I had done the first time I directly asked for someone's forgiveness. All I remember is how surprisingly *hard* it was. My outer appearance may have been calm, but inside I felt like I was delivering my first public speech. "If I have to go through this every time I repent to someone, I may not make it" was my initial response; I was a rookie at wrongdoing repair, but I did learn and it did get easier.

SIX

Making Repairs at Home, in Church, on the Job

A T A RECENT WEDDING RECEPTION I studied the ballroom dancing styles of several people to see if I could pick up any pointers (my wife was getting tired of my "two-step shuffle"). It was entertaining. When the band struck up a waltz or a polka, many of the couples seemed to lose their bearings. One dancing pair would try a few steps (which were less than fluid), stop for a brief consultation with each other, and take another disjointed stab at it. Another fellow was barking orders to his bewildered partner: *right*-two-three-*left*-two-three. Then I noticed a retired fire chief and his elderly wife weaving adroitly through the struggling throng of neophytes. Heads even, legs and feet moving in near perfect unison—they made it look easy. Turning to my wife, I asked, "Why don't we look like that?" The expression on her face said it all: "*They* dance the same dance when they dance."

Like dancing, repairing wrongdoing goes more smoothly when all parties involved are using the same technique. In other words, a biblical approach to repairing wrongdoing works best when it is a common approach.

The New Testament teaching on repairing wrongdoing was intended to be just that: a common approach for a group of Christians seeking to maintain Christian unity. Jesus' instructions were given to those who would become the first Christian community, and Paul's instructions were addressed to local bodies of committed Christians. We need to take this fact into account when we try to put a Christian approach to repairing wrongdoing into practice. First of all, we should pay special attention to practicing wrongdoing repair in groups where it is possible to have a common approach. The family and the local church or Christian group are two important places where a common approach to wrongdoing repair can be practiced. Second, wisdom will be needed for applying a Christian approach to wrongdoing repair when there is no consensus about how wrongdoing should be handled.

Home Repairs

Most of the wrong things I've done have either taken place in my own home or involved members of my family. As examples of your own wrongdoing have come to mind, you've probably noticed the same trend. The home is an ideal place to practice wrongdoing repair.

Husband and Wife. I've had occasion to counsel married couples on the verge of divorce. As they unravel intricate stories of frustration and misunderstanding, two glaring inadequacies emerge in almost every case. First, the marriage is characterized by poor communication, a problem about which marriage counsellors and psychologists have written at great length. Second, at least one of the partners has committed acts of wrongdoing against the other which have never been repaired. Sometimes the wrongdoing is serious—like adultery. But often they are a collection of less serious wrongs, which after festering like so many pockets of unattended infection, have just as devastating an effect. These are the kinds of wrongdoing which can occur in any marriage—unkept promises, irresponsibility, misplaced anger, irritability. Whether wrongdoing is large or small, it will have serious consequences in any marriage if it is not repaired. The popular expression "Love means never having to say you're sorry" is harmless enough when restricted to posters and greeting cards, but when taken seriously, it is an invitation to disaster.

It isn't enough for married couples to agree in principle on the importance of repairing wrongdoing. They should agree on the specific approach they will use to repair it. In our early years of marriage, my wife and I agreed that we shouldn't "sweep things under the rug," but we didn't have any specific understanding of what to do instead. Every now and then Nancy would be upset about something I had done a few days previously. "But I thought we already took care of that," I would reply incredulously. I was referring, of course, to my mumbled apology and my attempts to be extra nice to her. "I didn't know you were apologizing," Nancy would reply. Then we would take another stab at it.

It is also necessary to discuss those grey areas—things which are on the borderline or in a questionable category. Some people think of them as wrong, others think of them as "not so good." Whenever possible, it is best to agree on whether to handle them as wrongdoing or not. For example, I thought that an occasional swat on the behind or a surprise pinch was "just being playful" with Nancy. She thought it was being disrespectful. We talked about it and agreed on what was disrespectful.

If a couple has not been practicing wrongdoing repair, it may take some extra effort and resources to get started. Old habits of handling wrongdoing in marriage will not be broken overnight. After agreeing on a common approach, a husband and wife will also need to remind one another about practicing it when opportunities arise. If a wife repents to her husband for being grouchy and irritable with him and he replies with the habitual "Oh don't worry about it," she might reply, "But it was wrong—that's why I'm asking you to forgive me. What do you say?"

Some couples may need outside help to deal with instances of wrongdoing which have been particularly damaging, especially when they have been covered over for years. It may be hard for one partner to forgive another or to have any expectation that a pattern of wrong behavior will change. The wrongdoing may be tangled in a web of emotional factors which make it more difficult to deal with. In these cases, a respected counsellor may be needed to help clear up confusion from the past and provide a strategy for the future.

Teaching Children to Repair Wrongdoing. Teaching children how to handle wrongdoing is an important part of raising them "in the Lord." I have found that children can begin to practice the steps involved in repairing wrongdoing at a very early age.

Like much that is learned, learning to repent and be reconciled begins at a very basic, even mechanical level. Children need firm, simple, on-the-spot instruction. For example, when one of my younger children disobeys me, I will require him to say, "I was wrong to disobey you, Dad. Please forgive me." Especially when some form of punishment is necessary, expressing forgiveness and providing some physical affection brings the matter to an end.

As children grow older, their capacity for repentance matures. At first, the younger ones realize only that when they do something wrong they should ask for something called "forgiveness." They know that after they receive forgiveness, the issue is settled. But as they mature, they need to learn that wrongdoing consists of more than whatever displeases Mom or Dad. It is based on an objective standard set by the Lord. They need to learn that they have an ability to make decisions, and that they must exercise that ability in order to turn away from wrongdoing. They should also learn that sorrow for sin is more than just sorrow for the consequences of getting caught.

Consistency is important. Children should learn that the various steps of wrongdoing repair need to be taken *whenever* we do something wrong. It is not reserved for the most serious offenses or for those which happen to bother the parent. Nor is this method of repairing wrongdoing reserved for children, to be shed for more sophisticated methods later in life. Children also need to see that the process works in reverse. For instance, when parents react out of misdirected anger or irritation, or when they fail to keep their word to their children, they ought to repent and seek forgiveness from the child. (This not only keeps the relationship with the children clear, but also sets an example for them and teaches them that repentance is for adults, too.)

The other day, my oldest son came home angry because he had been to a friend's house and was told to wait for the friend in his bedroom. After a forty-five minute wait, he realized that he was the only one left in the house. His friend's mother, harried with a number of the neighbor's children to care for, had apparently forgotten about him and left the house. When my son told me about the situation, I said, "If you have a grievance, you should talk to your friend's mother about it." Fortunately she was a very gracious Christian woman. Though it was a borderline case (she wasn't sure that she had been informed that he was waiting in the bedroom), I think she realized that this would be a good lesson for my son in handling wrongdoing. So she graciously asked for my son's forgiveness. When I heard of his wide-eyed response to her request over the phone and his somewhat surprised "I forgive you," I knew that he had learned an important lesson about handling wrongdoing.

To make a lasting impression, wrongdoing repair must be applied in all sorts of situations—when children disobey their parents, when they wrong one of their friends or siblings, when they are wronged by others, including their parents, or when they do something wrong which only affects their relationship with God.

Two Pitfalls. When teaching children to repent and seek forgiveness, parents should avoid two particular pitfalls. The first concerns how the child experiences guilt feelings. The effect of repentance and reconciliation should be to free children from guilt, not to burden them with excessive guilt feelings. When I correct one of my children I make a point to say, "What you did was wrong," rather than, "You are a bad boy for doing that." (Eventually the children need to learn that what scripture calls the "old man" *is* utterly corrupt—a bad boy if there ever was one. But making them feel bad about themselves is not the best way to accomplish this.) If, after repenting, I sense that the child is still feeling bad, I may add a brief teaching about forgiveness and guilt feelings: "You've been forgiven, so that means it's over and done with—let's both forget about it and be thankful that the Lord loves us enough to want to make us like himself."

The second pitfall might be called "dead-letter repentance." It happens when children merely go through the motions of wrongdoing repair without meaning or understanding what they are doing. While it is helpful to have a method for expressing repentance, the method cannot replace conviction on the child's part.

When my daughter was about five years old, she went through a "disrespectful" phase. She repented a number of times for being disrespectful when I corrected her, but it was obvious that she was not catching on. Finally I asked her, "Do you know what is wrong with being disrespectful?"

"I don't know," she replied with a corresponding shrug. She was obviously going through the motions of repentance without the personal conviction that disrespectful behavior was wrong. It was time for some simple instruction, but how does one explain to a five-year-old what is wrong with being disrespectful? Before boarding the "But *why*, Daddy?" merry-go-round, I gave it some careful thought and tried to keep it simple. "God wants us to show respect to him and to show respect to other people. When we interrupt people or don't say hello to them, we are acting disrespectfully, even if we don't mean to be disrespectful.

That's just the way it is. Being disrespectful is wrong because God doesn't like it. If we're smart, we'll do it his way." My daughter was smart enough to know that it's wrong to do things God doesn't like; her subsequent repentance has been more meaningful and more effective.

Church Repairs

The local church ought to be a place where people learn how to repair wrongdoing. Yet modern Christians may run into problems when they try to apply the biblical teaching in their relationships with Christians in their churches. These problems have two sources. First, many church groups don't follow a biblical approach, whether it is the approach described in this book or some other approach based on the biblical teaching. Even if it is taught from the pulpit, when it comes to individual instances of wrongdoing between members of a congregation, people often resort to the variety of approaches that prevail in society at large.

Second, many churches are not built upon committed personal relationships. Church members may maintain only limited commitment to one another. If they run into enough problems with people in one church, they may just choose another. And some church members are so insulated from other members that they don't even have the opportunity to wrong them.

Ideally, the church should be a place where

wrongdoing repair is taught and practiced within the context of committed personal relationships. The biblical approach would be the common approach, understood and practiced by the majority of Christians. New Christians wouldn't learn about repairing wrongdoing from books like this. They would learn from the examples of brothers and sisters and by instruction and observation.

Unfortunately, we are living in a time when much that is basic to Christian teaching needs to be restored, relearned, and reapplied. Inasmuch as our churches don't function as bodies of committed brothers and sisters with a common approach to repairing wrongdoing, the wisdom needed for applying this approach will be similar to the wisdom needed for repairing wrongdoing with those who are not Christians, which I will discuss later.

At the same time, groups of Christians can agree together to adopt a common approach to repairing wrongdoing. Then they can help each other put it into practice. But it takes more than an occasional sermon or a seminar on repairing wrongdoing. In order to apply the biblical approach successfully a few preconditions are necessary.

First, people in the group must desire to move their Christian lives forward. If they are complacent or uninterested, nothing will happen. The solution to lack of interest is personal spiritual renewal. No teaching about how to live a Christian life will be effective until people are *motivated* to live a Christian life.

Second, members of the group must be committed to loving one another. The relationships must be characterized by an underlying commitment to care for and serve one another. People must desire right relationships deeply enough to invest the necessary time to overcome the difficulties they may encounter as they work through problems in their relationships.

Third, to take on the biblical approach to repairing wrongdoing, people must have enough opportunity to put it into practice. If their only contact with each other is an hour on Sunday, they won't have enough of a relationship to damage. Though all Christian bodies need to hear about repairing wrongdoing, the groups most able to receive this teaching and put it into practice are ones in which the members already relate to one another regularly: the staff of a church, the leaders' team for a prayer group, a board of deacons or elders, or other situations in which Christians live or serve together or care for each other in a committed way.

When Others Do It Differently

Suppose you insult a co-worker who is not a Christian, or who has no understanding of the Christian way of repairing wrongdoing. When you go to him and say, "Bob, I was wrong to insult you the other day. Will you forgive me?" you might elicit a variety of responses beyond a simple yes or no. Of course he might startle you and say, "I forgive you." But he might also shrug it off with an, "Oh, that was nothing—forget it." He might say, "As long as you were being sincere, you don't have to regret anything you said." Or he might respond, "Saying you're sorry doesn't *change anything*." Or, "you should have thought of that before you said it—too late now."

Two principles should guide our attempts to repair wrongdoing with those who approach it differently than we do. First, the *goal* is reconciliation, or peaceful relationships. (This is limited by the fact that reconciliation with those who are not brothers and sisters in Christ may sometimes not be possible.) St. Paul stated this goal clearly when he wrote, "If possible, so far as it depends on you, be at peace with all men" (Rom 12:8). Second, while the biblical approach is the best method since it reflects God's wisdom, it may be necessary to adapt it for use with those who don't follow it. In some cases, applying a biblical standard for the way others handle wrongdoing may work against the goal of reconciliation instead of for it. This does not mean that we should be apologetic about the Christian approach, or automatically abandon it when others around us don't live by it. In fact, in many situations it is best to apply the biblical approach without adaptation. But we should also be free to adapt the approach when it would serve the goal of reconciliation.

These two principles provide the basis for the following guidelines for repairing wrongdoing with those who do it differently.

1. *When you've done something wrong, follow the biblical approach as much as possible, whether or not it's expected of you.* In some settings, it's normal for people to wrong each other without repairing the damage. Consequently they learn not to expect much from each other. But standards for our behavior shouldn't change from one environment to the next. By setting a good example, we can influence the way others handle their wrongdoing.

2. *Avoid religious language.* Terms which are understood only in Christian environments should be avoided. The word "repent" is a good example. Someone who hears you say, "I repent for the way I treated you," will probably think that you are taking things much too seriously, or that you are just "doing something religious." Use terms that the other person can understand.

3. *Don't expect someone who is not a Christian to respond as a Christian should.* We should not be scandalized if we seek forgiveness and are refused. Even many Christians have difficulty forgiving one another, and they have a greater resource than those who are not Christians! A person may need time to let an issue "settle down." If he or she flatly refuses to forgive us, we can still be satisfied that in seeking forgiveness we have done our part. We are not responsible for the other person's response.

4. *Be gracious with those who are doing a sloppy job of repairing wrongdoing.* When a co-worker or

neighbor wrongs you, regrets it later, and comes to work it out with you, it is not necessary to hold that person to a Christian standard for repairing the wrong. Perhaps he has swallowed just enough of his pride to say, "Hey, I didn't mean to mess you up the other day." Rather than trying to coax him toward the four steps of wrongdoing, you might reply, "I'm not perfect either, so I won't hold it against you."

This doesn't mean we should always be easygoing when it comes to the wrong actions of others. If the office gossip spreads some damaging rumors about you and then says, "Oh, I know that I can't keep my mouth shut sometimes; I really should be more careful," you may want to respond, "I don't think you understand the problem you caused me. I want you to stop gossiping about me, and I think a serious apology is in order."

Fortunately, in many cultures the Christian approach to repairing wrongdoing is respected even if it isn't practiced. It contains elements which people instinctively admire: honesty, directness, and simple social courage. Even if they can't bring themselves to adopt it, most people will respect the person who practices it.

Conclusion

AS A YOUNG CANDIDATE for confirmation, a friend of mine somehow got the impression that after confirmation he would never sin again. He thought it was part of a package deal that came with being a Christian. After he was confirmed, experience quickly taught him that he had not become invulnerable to wrongdoing. This self-discovery prompted him to conclude that the whole thing was a hoax, and he gave up on Christianity for a few years. Many of us are just a bit surprised and perhaps disappointed to find that we haven't been wrapped up in cellophane and sent straight to heaven after seriously committing our lives to Christ. But the Lord doesn't guarantee instantaneous perfection, nor does he provide cellophane to wrap us up and ship us off with. Instead, he releases us from the domination of sin and gives us a foretaste of the life of the age to come, in which wrongdoing will no longer exist. In the meantime he provides wisdom for handling the wrongs we commit. Until the new order of the kingdom of heaven has swept the old order aside completely, that wisdom will provide us with an invaluable tool, a tool that can repair damage which might otherwise undo us.

Notes

1. See Bert Ghezzi, *The Angry Christian* (Ann Arbor, Michigan: Servant Books, 1980).

2. Knight-Ridder Newspapers.

3. See Mark Kinzer, *The Self-Image of a Christian* (Ann Arbor, Michigan: Servant Books, 1980) for an excellent treatment of sorrow and self-condemnation.

The books in the *Living as a Christian* series can be used effectively in groups. To receive a free copy of the Leader's Guide to this book and the others in the series, send a stamped, self-addressed business envelope to Servant Books, Box 8617, Ann Arbor, Michigan 48107.